The Don't Laugh™ Challenge

Dad vs. Kid

· Edition ·

DLC Triple Play + Bonus

Join our joke club and get the
DLC Triple Play + Bonus.

Simply send us an email at
bacchuspublish@gmail.com
and you get the following:

1. Secret Top 10 List of Never Seen Before Jokes!

2. EXTRA round of our Word Frenzy!

3. EXTRA round of our Silly Scenarios!

Bonus

You get entered into a drawing to win a signed copy
of our next book by Billy Boy -
Personalized to YOU!

We draw a new winner each month!

Welcome to
The Don't Laugh Challenge™

• How do you play?

The Don't Laugh Challenge is made up of 10 rounds with 3 games in each round. It is a 2-3 player game with the players being 'Dad', 'Kid', and/or another player. In each game you have an opportunity to score points by making the other players laugh.

After completing each round, tally up the points to determine the Round Champion! Add all 10 rounds together to see who is the Ultimate Don't Laugh Challenge Master! If you end up in a tie, use our final Tie Breaker Round for a Winner Takes All!

Who can play the game?

• Get the whole family involved! Grab a family member or a friend and take turns going back and forth. We've also added Bonus Points in game 3, so grab a 3rd person, and earn an extra point by making them guess your scene!

The Don't Laugh Challenge ™
Activity Rules

- ## Game 1 - Jokes (1 point each)

  Dad will hold the book and read each joke to Kid. If the joke makes Kid laugh, Dad can record a point for the joke. Each joke is worth 1 point. At the end of the jokes, tally up your total Joke Points scored for Dad and continue to Game 2!

- ## Game 2 - Word Frenzy (2 points each)

  To begin, Dad will call out a part of speech for Kid to answer (like adjective or verb). Next, Dad will record the answers to complete the sentences. Continue until all blanks are filled, but without reading any of the sentences out loud yet! Once ALL of the answers are recorded in the blank spaces, read the completed sentences out loud to Kid. If you make the Kid laugh with your crazy sentences, record your points. Tally up your Word Frenzy Points at the bottom and continue on to Game 3!

  A little help if you need it:

  Noun = person, place or thing.

  Adjective = a descriptive word that describes a noun.

  Adverb = modifies another verb or adjective.

  Proper Noun = person place or thing that starts with a capital letter.

8

The Don't Laugh Challenge ™
Activity Rules

Game 3 - Silly Scenarios
(2 points each + bonus point)

Read the scenario to yourself then act it out. You can use sound effects, but be sure not to say any words! Make the other person laugh and score two points!

Bonus Point:
Get your parents or a third player involved and have them guess the scene. If they guess correctly, the person scores a bonus point!

After Dad completes their 3 games it is Kid's turn. Follow the directions at the bottom of each page if you get stuck. Once all the games have been completed in the round, add up your points and record the round winner!

How do you get started?
Hand the book to Dad to start the first round.

Tip: Make any of the activities extra funny by using facial expressions, funny voices or silly movements!

ROUND
1

Dad goes first!

Dad Jokes

DAD

What's better than good cheese?

Grate cheese.   /1

What do you get when you cross
a pit-bull with a comforter?

A security blanket.
                                                           /1

What pastry gets picked on the
most?

Shortbread.
                                                           /1

Why did the family gather on the
beach?

They wanted to see the CURRENT   /1
event!

JOKES TOTAL: _____ /4

Dad continue to the next page ➡

Word Frenzy

DAD

1. Noun (Animal)
2. Noun (Snack - Plural)
3. Noun (Plural)

I used to want to be a(n) _____, but then I found out that you
                        #1
can't eat _____ in the wild. Now, I'm happy to be a human,
          #2
so I can enjoy my salty _____. That's my favorite snack!
                         #3

/2

1. Proper Noun (Famous Person)
2. Verb (Ends in ING)
3. Verb (Ends in ED)

Last night, my wife and I spotted _____ _____
                                        #1   #2
outside of a restaurant. My wife ran over to get his/her

autograph, but was so nervous she couldn't speak and then she

_____. I acted like I didn't know her and walked away.
   #3

/2

WORD FRENZY TOTAL: _____ /4

Dad continue to the next page ➡

Silly Scenarios

You're in the middle of giving a haircut, when the customer sneezes. Now they have a bald spot! Try to glue their hair back on without them noticing!

_____ /2

You are a snake that swallows a huge rat. Work the huge rat through your mouth, down your throat, and to your knees (the snake's stomach), using only your slimy snake ability to squirm your food through your body!

_____ /2

SILLY SCENARIOS TOTAL: _____ /4

Now, pass the book to Kid!

Kid Jokes

What's orange and flat?

An orange that got run over.

_____ /1

Why did the car go to sleep?

Because it was TIRE-d.

_____ /1

Why does O always look at P's homework?

Because he is a Cheat-O.

_____ /1

Why did the nose dance so well?

He had the boogie in him!

_____ /1

JOKES TOTAL: _____ /4

Kid continue to the next page ➡

Word Frenzy

1. Proper Noun (Famous Person)
2. Noun (Plural)
3. Noun (Body part)
4. Noun (Vegetable)

_____ had a fall from grace and was the magician for my
#1

friend's birthday party. He/She was actually pretty good!

He/She made all of the _____ disappear and turned Joey's
#2

_____ into a _____. I think he/she is on his/her
#3   #4

way to a major comeback!

_____ /2

1. Proper Noun (Friends Name - Male)
2. Verb (Ends in ING)
3. Noun (Animal)

My friend, _____, used to be very popular until some kids
#1

walked in on him _____ with his pet _____. What
#2   #3

made it worse was that he wasn't even embarrassed, but actually

kind of proud!

_____ /2

WORD FRENZY TOTAL: _____ /4

Kid continue to the next page ➔

Silly Scenarios

Pretend to blow a GIANT bubble, that explodes and sticks to every part of your body!

_____ /2

There is an alien creature that snuck under your covers and attached itself to your back. It starts to take control of your body and move around. This alien loves to dance!

_____ /2

SILLY SCENARIOS TOTAL: _____ /4

 **DAD** **/12**

GRAND TOTAL

 **KID** **/12**

GRAND TOTAL

ROUND CHAMPION

ROUND 2

Pass the book to Dad!

Dad Jokes

Why do you need sunglasses to go birdwatching?

___/1

Because their feathers are so light.

Why are football players allowed to play catch in the hall?

They're using a hall pass.

___/1

People who love selling phones must have really found their calling.

___/1

Why did the battery feel so drained after a day in court?

___/1

He wasn't charged with a crime.

JOKES TOTAL: ___ /4

Dad continue to the next page

Word Frenzy

DAD

1. Noun (Plural)
2. Adjective

As I was walking into the pharmacy yesterday, I was shocked

to see a group of doctors running out the store carrying

_____! They had a(n)_____ look in their eyes. I don't
#1 #2

know where I'm going to go when I get sick again, but it won't be

their hospital!

_____ /2

1. Proper Noun (Friend's Name - Female)
2. Noun (Animal - Plural)
3. Noun (Animal - Plural)
4. Proper Noun (Famous Person)

My friend,_____, is a very stylish person. She usually
#1

wears a big coat made from _____ and shoes made from
#2

_____. Some people think she hates animals, but I think
#3

she just wants to be like _____.
#4

_____ /2

WORD FRENZY TOTAL: _____ /4

Dad continue to the next page ➡

Silly Scenarios

DAD

You just realized that your flying chicken lays golden eggs! They are very fragile and completely fall apart if they hit the ground. Catch the next six as your chicken flies around the room!

_____ /2

You're in a boat and it's quickly taking in water! HURRY! Grab a straw and drink as much as you can, so you don't sink!

_____ /2

SILLY SCENARIOS TOTAL: _____ /4

Now, pass the book to Kid!

Kid Jokes

Why did no one trust the cell phone?
It was acting phony.

/1

What did the landing say to the steps?
"What are you STAIR-ing at?"

/1

What kind of pie does a comedian bring to Thanksgiving dinner?
PUN-kin.

/1

Why are umpires always sick?
They keep catching colds.

/1

JOKES TOTAL: _____ /4

Kid continue to the next page ➡

Word Frenzy

1. Proper Noun (Country, outside of the U.S.)
2. Noun (Animal - Plural)
3. Noun (Article of Clothing - Plural)
4. Noun - (Animal)

Yesterday, all of _____ lost its power. It didn't take long fo
#1
society to breakdown. There were wild _____ running the
#2
streets, and old women were even trading their favorite

_____ for fried _____ ! It was madness!
#3   #4

_____ /2

1. Proper Noun (Friend's Name - Male)
2. Adjective
3. Noun (Vegetable - Plural)
4. Noun

_____ looked so embarrassed and slightly _____ , as he
#1   #2
watched his dad juggle _____ for his work's talent show.
#3
After it was over, he gave his son a huge _____ to get back
#4
in his good graces. Some things just aren't worth it!

_____ /2

WORD FRENZY TOTAL: _____ /4

Kid continue to the next page ➡

28

Silly Scenarios

The Big Bad Wolf has come to you for lessons on how to huff and puff. Show him your secret technique for blowing houses down!

_____ /2

You're a marathon runner about to break the ribbon across the finish line and celebrate the end of the race! When you try to break the ribbon, you keep bouncing back. Keeping trying until it breaks!

_____ /2

SILLY SCENARIOS TOTAL: _____ /4

 DAD /12
GRAND TOTAL

 KID /12
GRAND TOTAL

ROUND
CHAMPION

ROUND
3

Pass the book to Dad!

Dad Jokes

Why couldn't the chef get any soup at the store?

_____ /1

They were out of stock.

A human and a cigar had a race. Who won?

The cigar. The human smoked him.

_____ /1

What type of shampoo are fish unable to use?

Head and Shoulders.

_____ /1

What does a cat call a lizard that can't change color?

"Dinner."

_____ /1

JOKES TOTAL: _____ /4

Dad continue to the next page

Word Frenzy

DAD

1. Noun (Animal)
2. Adjective
3. Adjective
4. Adjective

Yesterday, I saw a(n)_____ in my backyard. It was _____
      #1   #2
and _____. I tried to catch it in a trap, but I was too slow
      #3
and it was too_____. I will be ready for it next time!
               #4

_____ /2

1. Adjective
2. Noun (Animal)
3. Adjective

I went for a haircut, but the barber was_____. When he
                                              #1
was finished, I felt like I looked like a(n)_____! I was
                                              #2
so embarrassed, but all the kids at school thought I looked

_____. Within a week, everyone in my class had the same
   #3
haircut!

_____ /2

WORD FRENZY TOTAL: _____ /4

Dad continue to the next page ➡

Silly Scenarios

DAD

You're running a marathon, but instead of running shoes, you decided to run in ice skates! Good luck!

_____ /2

You're a robot. Uh-oh, someone spilled water on you and you begin to short-circuit and act crazy!

_____ /2

SILLY SCENARIOS TOTAL: _____ /4

Now, pass the book to Kid!

Kid Jokes

What do you call a stinky
computer?

A com-PEE-YU-ter.   /1

Knock knock.
Who's there?
Yaw.
Yaw who?
Well, you're excited to see me!   /1

Where do comedian's go to eat
their lunch?

The Laugh-eteria.   /1

Why can't the lazy racecar driver
win any races?

Because he's got no drive.   /1

JOKES TOTAL: _____ /4

Kid continue to the next page ➡

Word Frenzy

1. Noun (Animal)
2. Noun (Amusement Park Ride)

Last year, I got a miniature _____ for Christmas. It was so
#1

small that I didn't even know what to do with it, so I let my sister

play with it. She built it a Lego _____ and sings to it each
#2

night before bed. I guess I won't be getting it back anytime soon

_____ /2

1. Verb (Ends in ING)
2. Verb
3. Noun (Body part)

Dad and I went for a walk on the beach, but the sand was so hot

we started_____! People were cringing at the sight, so
#1

we decided we should _____ instead! It wasn't long befor
#2

the lifeguard came down and gave us a ride on his _____
#3

back to the house. Next time, we will definitely wear sandals!

_____ /2

WORD FRENZY TOTAL: _____ /4

Kid continue to the next page ➡

Silly Scenarios

It's Halloween, but every piece of candy that you eat makes your legs stop working. Try to crawl to the rest of the candy, without using your legs!

_____ /2

You are a unicorn who paints portraits, using only your horn. Now paint a picture of your Dad!

_____ /2

SILLY SCENARIOS TOTAL: _____ /4

DAD

/12

GRAND TOTAL

KID

/12

GRAND TOTAL

ROUND
CHAMPION

ROUND

4

Pass the book to Dad!

Dad Jokes

DAD

What's the best job for cheaters?

Copywriting. /1

Why are baseball player's so good at science?

They have a lot to BASE their evidence on. /1

What do you do if you see a bee that looks like John Lennon?

Let it Bee. /1

Why was the dinosaur never on time?

He came from the late Jurassic period. /1

JOKES TOTAL: /4

Dad continue to the next page →

Word Frenzy

DAD

1. Noun (Insect - Plural)
2. Noun (Plural)

Every night before bed, I eat ten _____. They make me fee
$\qquad$ #1

like I can leap over 100 _____ in a single bound! My Mom
$\qquad$ #2

says it's disgusting, but who else do you know that can do that?

____/2

1. Proper Noun (Famous Actress)
2. Noun (Animal)
3. Noun (Place)
4. Noun (Type of Weapon - Plural)

Last summer, I saw a YouTube video with _____
$\qquad$ #1

saying she saw a(n) _____ in the _____ by
$\qquad$ #2 $\qquad$ #3

her house. I am not sure if I believe her, but if I saw one near

my house, I'd hope to have _____ to protect myself
$\qquad$ #4

No such thing as being too careful!

____/2

WORD FRENZY TOTAL: ____ /4

Dad continue to the next page ➡

44

Silly Scenarios

Dinnertime is over and you throw the dishes into the dishwasher; inside the dishwasher are little people who clean the dishes. Today, you're one of those little people. Start cleaning!

_____ /2

You're a sloth, who plays basketball. Try and get a slam dunk... in SLOW MOTION!

_____ /2

SILLY SCENARIOS TOTAL: _____ /4

STOP

Now, pass the book to Kid!

Kid Jokes

Why does the baker always tease his dough?
He's trying to get a rise out of it!

___ /1

Why can't scales take bad news?
It's usually too heavy.

___ /1

What did one scarecrow say to the other?
"HAY!"

___ /1

Why are doorknobs so good at board games?
It's always their turn.

___ /1

JOKES TOTAL: ___ /4

Kid continue to the next page ➡

Word Frenzy

KID

1. Noun (Animal)
2. Noun (Animal - Plural)
3. Noun (Type of Food - Plural)

Last year on a hike up Mt. Crested Butte, Dad reached the summit

and yelled, "_____, _____, _____" at the
                        #1   #1   #1

top of his lungs. I was excited too, but that seemed weird to yell.

He must be like Snow White because the next thing I know, all the

_____ started coming out of the bushes with a hungry look in
       #2

their eyes. Fortunately, we had some _____ to feed them and
                                                    #3

keep them at bay. We won't be doing that hike again anytime soon

_____ /2

1. Noun (Animal)
2. Noun (Thing)
3. Noun (Body Part)

I'll never bring my pet _____ to school again! It ruined my
                                    #1

_____ and almost ate my best friend's _____ ! Talk about
       #2   #3

a mess... I still love it though!

_____ /2

WORD FRENZY TOTAL: _____ /4

Kid continue to the next page ➡

48

Silly Scenarios

The Annual Watermelon Seed-Spitting Contest is tomorrow, and you're going to stay up all night practicing. Eat the watermelon without your hands and practice your pretend spitting!

_____ /2

You're chewing bubble gum and every time you blow a bubble, you start to float away! Keep blowing bubbles!

_____ /2

SILLY SCENARIOS TOTAL: _____ /4

 DAD $\dfrac{}{}$ /12

GRAND TOTAL

 KID $\dfrac{}{}$ /12

GRAND TOTAL

ROUND CHAMPION

ROUND 5

Pass the book to Dad!

Dad Jokes

DAD

Why was the farmer's best subject Geometry?

Because he was pro-TRACTOR.

/1

What do you call basil in a Christmas card?

Seasonings Greetings!

/1

What do you call the President during their Independence Day barbecue?

The Commander-in-Chef.

/1

What did the camel say, when he got stranded in the desert?

"Dune, where's my car?"

/1

JOKES TOTAL: _____ /4

Dad continue to the next page ➡

Word Frenzy

DAD

1. Noun (Thing)
2. Noun (Vegetable or Fruit – Plural)
3. Noun (Animal)
4. Proper Noun (Friend's Name)

There was a strange troll that lived under a(n)_____ in ou
#1

neighborhood, when I was growing up. His face reminded me of

mix between a(n)_____ and a(n)_____, kind of like _____
#2   #3   #4

At least he was friendly!

_____ /2

1. Proper Noun (Country, outside of the U.S.)
2. Noun (Animal - Plural)
3. Verb (Ends in ING)

Every time I go to _____, I always try to find some carame
#1

covered _____ meat. It's hard to find, but if you stand at a
#2

busy street corner _____, eventually, you will be led into a
#3

secret store where all the caramel covered meats are!

_____ /2

WORD FRENZY TOTAL: _____ /4

Dad continue to the next page ➡

Silly Scenarios

DAD

Pretend that you're trying to eat a sandwich, but you can't bend your elbows!

_____ /2

You have T-Rex arms and are attempting to play baseball! Show us your best swing!

_____ /2

SILLY SCENARIOS TOTAL: _____ /4

STOP

Now, pass the book to Kid!

Kid Jokes

What do you call a gymnast who cuts down trees?

A LIMBER-jack.   ___/1

How do you know wheels are a bad gift?

They're always getting returned.   ___/1

What do you call it when athletes pretend to be babies?

Playing bawl!   ___/1

What did the Snowboarder say after falling off of the chairlift?

"Looks like it's all downhill from here!"   ___/1

JOKES TOTAL: ___/4

Kid continue to the next page ➡

Word Frenzy

KID

1. Proper Noun (City)
2. Adjective
3. Noun (Animal - Plural)

Last year, while exploring the city streets of _____, we

fell in a hole that took us to the middle of Earth! Luckily, we were

kept safe by a group of _____, _____ who lived

                                              #2   #3

there. They were wonderful hosts, but we got out of there as

fast as we could!

_____ /2

1. Proper Noun (Famous Politician)
2. Noun (Animal)
3. Noun (Animal - Plural)
4. Proper Noun (Famous Politician)

Tomorrow, I go back to school and _____ is going to be

                                        #1

visiting with his/her pet _____, mixed with _____

                                  #2   #3

Apparently, he/she doesn't travel with it very often since it bit

_____ on his/her last visit. It's probably just politics,

#4

though!

_____ /2

WORD FRENZY TOTAL: _____ /4

Kid continue to the next page ➡

58

Silly Scenarios

KID

You're a robot trying to do the worm!

_____ /2

You're hoola hooping, but as you get going, the hoop catches on fire! Now you have have to go super fast and blow on it to put it out!

_____ /2

SILLY SCENARIOS TOTAL: _____ /4

 DAD _____ /12

GRAND TOTAL

 KID _____ /12

GRAND TOTAL

_____

ROUND CHAMPION

ROUND 6

Pass the book to Dad!

Dad Jokes

DAD

Why did Elsa need help with her computer?

It was frozen.

/1

Why did the tennis players get in trouble at school?

They were making a racket!

/1

What did the fungus say about their new apartment?

"There isn't mush-room!"

/1

Broken door companies are always successful, Just look at them, their doors are NEVER closing!

/1

JOKES TOTAL: ____ /4

Dad continue to the next page ➔

Word Frenzy

DAD

1. Proper Noun (Name - Male)
2. Verb
3. Adjective
4. Noun (Thing)

_____, the Wonder Dog, was the most amazing dog in
#1

the world! He could even _____ better than any human
#2

alive! Sometimes he wears a(n) _____ mask and tricks
#3

people into thinking he's a(n) _____. That always makes him
#4

wag his tail in delight!

_____ /2

1. Proper Noun (Country, outside of the U.S.)
2. Proper Noun (Friend's Name - Male)
3. Verb

I drove across the country of _____ and along my
#1

journey, I met a cowboy named _____. He used to
#2

_____ professionally, but now spends his time as a rodeo
#3

clown. Not the career move I would have imagined!

_____ /2

WORD FRENZY TOTAL: _____ /4

Dad continue to the next page ➡

Silly Scenarios

DAD

You have a pet porcupine that loves to snuggle. Demonstrate what it's like to snuggle and get pricked by your porcupine, but without making a noise!

_____ /2

You're so tired and want to sit down, but every time you try to, you sit on a nail. OUCH! Keep trying!

_____ /2

SILLY SCENARIOS TOTAL: _____ /4

Now, pass the book to Kid!

Kid Jokes

I played a basketball game with my alarm. It wasn't easy going against the clock!

_____ /1

What did the ocean say at the crime scene?

"Nothing to SEA here."

_____ /1

I've never seen a cloud win a fight against the wind, they always lose in a single blow.

_____ /1

What does a bodybuilder use for his hair?

A curling iron.

_____ /1

JOKES TOTAL: _____ /4

Kid continue to the next page

Word Frenzy

KID

1. Noun (Body Part)
2. Noun (Vegetable – Plural)
3. Noun (Article of Clothing – Plural)
4. Noun (Type of Dessert)

Once a beanstalk grew as tall as my house! A huge bean fell

off and smacked my dad right on the _____! Mom ran

#1

outside and yelled, "Oh, _____!" She proceeded to taste the

#2

bean goo from his _____, and liked it so much that she

#3

made us bean _____ for dinner. I'm SO over beans!

#4

_____/2

1. Noun (Place)
2. Verb (Ends in S)
3. Noun (Plural)
4. Proper Noun (Friend's Name)
5. Noun (Plural)

When my Dad goes to the _____, he always _____

#1   #2

_____. Then yells for _____ to get him some

#3   #4

_____!

#5

_____/2

WORD FRENZY TOTAL: _____/4

Kid continue to the next page ➡

68

Silly Scenarios

You just had the sourest Sour Patch Kid EVER, and now have to take your school photo. Do your craziest, most sour face!

_____ /2

Your head is as heavy as a bowling ball. Try to hold it up with your hands as best as you can!

_____ /2

SILLY SCENARIOS TOTAL: _____ /4

 DAD   /12

GRAND TOTAL

 KID   /12

GRAND TOTAL

ROUND
CHAMPION

ROUND 7

Pass the book to Dad!

Dad Jokes

Why didn't Jupiter throw Saturn a birthday party?

He forgot to planet.

/1

How do you dress a carnivore?

In a skirt steak!

/1

When the doctor forgot his wallet at dinner, he asked if the restaurant would take check-ups.

/1

What do you call a photo of a coffee cup?

A mugshot.

/1

JOKES TOTAL: _____ /4

Dad continue to the next page →

Word Frenzy

DAD

1. Proper Noun (Friend's Name - Female)
2. Proper Noun (Place)
3. Verb (Ends in ING)
4. Adjective

_____ is going to be an important politician in the
#1

future. She is from _____ , and is always _____
#2   #3

for a good cause. I easily recognized her across the room in

her _____ hat.
#4

_____ /2

1. Proper Noun (Famous Person)
2. Noun (Animal)
3. Adjective
4. Verb

Last night, I was visited by aliens that all looked exactly the same

It reminded me of a cross between _____ and a(n) _____
#1   #2

They said they've chosen me because I'm _____ and I
#3

_____ well. We will see how this goes!
#4

_____ /2

WORD FRENZY TOTAL: _____ /4

Dad continue to the next page ➡

Silly Scenarios

Every step you take lands on a tiny LEGO.
Hop around to get away, but keep landing on
LEGO's. OUCH!

_____ /2

You're having a water balloon fight with friends,
except instead of water it is filled with acid. You
got hit and it BURNS! Slowly and dramatically, melt
down to the ground!

_____ /2

SILLY SCENARIOS TOTAL: _____ /4

Now, pass the book to Kid!

Kid Jokes

What did the skeptical artist say when someone told him to mix red and white?

"I don't PINK so!"

/1

What do you call a baseball made of money?

A Fare Ball.

/1

Did you hear about the professional bowling team asking for a raise?

I hear they're going on strike.

/1

Why are actors so good at connecting dots?

They remember all their lines.

/1

JOKES TOTAL: _____ /4

Kid continue to the next page

Word Frenzy

KID

1. Noun (Animal)
2. Proper Noun (Friend's Name)
3. Noun (Body Part)
4. Noun (Thing)

Last week after school, I reached my hand in my pocket and

pulled out a little _____. Its face was long and pointy like my
                         #1

friend, _____, and laughed when I tickled it's _____.
          #2   #3

When my mom came home later that evening, I hid it under my

_____. She'll never know about my tiny, new friend!
    #4

_____ /2

1. Proper Noun (Name)
2. Noun (Animal)
3. Verb (Ends in ED)

Dad loves to take the family to the farm. On our last visit, we

rode _____, our pet _____. Mom _____ with
              #1   #2   #3

rage when she found out! I guess not all pets are made to ride!

_____ /2

WORD FRENZY TOTAL: _____ /4

Kid continue to the next page ➡

78

Silly Scenarios

Your hands are glued together, but you have a basketball game. Try your best to play basketball, without separating your hands!

_____ /2

You are a spider and a bird gets caught in your web! Hurry and wrap him up, before he can eat you!

_____ /2

SILLY SCENARIOS TOTAL: _____ /4

DAD

/12

GRAND TOTAL

KID

/12

GRAND TOTAL

ROUND CHAMPION

ROUND
8

Pass the book to Dad!

Dad Jokes

DAD

How does the Psychic like her steak cooked?

Medium.

/1

What is the most confused monster?

A Where Wolf?!

/1

What do all elves want for Christmas?

A day off.

/1

I asked my friend if he knew any Braille and he said "just a touch."

/1

JOKES TOTAL: _____ /4

Dad continue to the next page

Word Frenzy

DAD

1. Verb
2. Adjective
3. Noun (Plural)

Alex used to _____ every time he heard the ice cream truc.
##1
but last week his vanilla cone was _____ . Since then, his
##2
taste buds have been off and now he prefers _____
##3
as his favorite snack!

_____ /2

1. Adjective
2. Noun (Animal)
3. Noun (Animal)
4. Proper Noun (Friend's Name)

While scuba diving last week, I saw a(n) _____ fish that
##1
had the face of a(n) _____ and the body of a(n) _____
##2   ##3
It reminded me of my friend, _____ . Nobody believes
##4
my story, but how can I make that up?!

_____ /2

WORD FRENZY TOTAL: _____ /4

Dad continue to the next page ➡

Silly Scenarios

DAD

Giving your best scared chicken impression, act like you are the first chicken in the world to ride a roller coaster!

_____ /2

You go to the beach, but the sand is quicksand! Quick, try to run! You're sinking!

_____ /2

SILLY SCENARIOS TOTAL: _____ /4

STOP

Now, pass the book to Kid!

Kid Jokes

Today was my first-day trying archery. I didn't know if I would be good at hitting targets, so I took a shot.

_____ /1

What did the light switch say when the lights were out?

"It's my day OFF!"

_____ /1

Why is butter so good at gambling?

It's usually on a roll.

_____ /1

What did the two baseball players say when they met up?

"Let's touch base soon!"

_____ /1

JOKES TOTAL: _____ /4

Kid continue to the next page ➔

Word Frenzy

1. Proper Noun (Country, outside of the U.S.)
2. Noun (Article of Clothing)
3. Noun (Article of Clothing)
4. Noun (Animal - Plural)

Next weekend, we're going to a park in _____ ! They have
#1

some strange rules, though. You have to wear _____ (s)
#2

on your feet and cover you face with a(n)_____ , so the loca
#3

_____ don't mistake you for prey. They must be pretty
#4

aggressive!

_____ /2

1. Noun
2. Verb (Past Tense)
3. Noun (Body Part)
4. Verb (Past Tense)

One day, Dad and I went to the foot spa. He loved the _____
#1

they gave him, but then they _____ every _____ .
#2   #3

He _____ and never went back.
#4

_____ /2

WORD FRENZY TOTAL: _____ /4

Kid continue to the next page ➔

Silly Scenarios

You're playing soccer, in cleats, on an ice rink.
Good luck, try not to fall repeatedly!

/2

Act like you are a Cuckoo Clock designed to spin
and burp every three seconds. 1...2...3... GO!

/2

SILLY SCENARIOS TOTAL: _____ /4

 DAD /12

GRAND TOTAL

 KID /12

GRAND TOTAL

ROUND CHAMPION

ROUND 9

Pass the book to Dad!

Dad Jokes

DAD

Did you hear about the dock who was trying to fit in with the other docks?

It was pier pressure.

/1

What's the only part of the hamburger the President needs to talk about?

The State of the Onion.

/1

Who wrote the fishes' Declaration of Independence?

The Floudering Fathers.

/1

How do you avoid an unwanted holiday kiss?

/1

Missile-toe!

JOKES TOTAL: /4

Dad continue to the next page

Word Frenzy

DAD

1. Noun (Body Part)
2. Noun (Thing)
3. Noun (Thing - Plural)
4. Noun (Animal)

Yesterday, I went to the doctor because I thought I broke my

_____, jumping from a(n)_____. The doctor told me to
    #1   #2

eat lots of _____, and wear lots of _____ oil to hide the
              #3   #4

smell of the cast, and that should help me heal faster!

/2

1. Adjective
2. Noun (Animal)
3. Proper Noun (Famous Person)
4. Noun (Thing - Plural)

I had a dream last night about a(n)_____ _____ who
                                      #1   #2

began committing crimes with _____. They stole all the
                                  #3

_____ across town, and were selling them back to the people
    #4

in town at ridiculously high prices! Good thing it was just a dream

/2

WORD FRENZY TOTAL: _____ /4

Dad continue to the next page ➡

94

Silly Scenarios

DAD

You're walking to school, but every step you take makes your bookbag heavier, and heavier, and HEAVIER! Good luck getting there!

_____ /2

This is your first mission in the space station and you're new to antigravity. You break your first meal pack open and have to float around gobbling up your food. Don't let any food get away!

_____ /2

SILLY SCENARIOS TOTAL: _____ /4

Now, pass the book to Kid!

Kid Jokes

KID

My favorite football team lost
their big game last night due to a
quiet crowd. They had no chants.   /1

What kind of insect breathes fire
when he's angry?
A DRAGON-fly!   /1

Why do teddy bears love buffets?
It's the best place to get stuffed!   /1

How do you break up with a
personal trainer?
Just say "We're not working out."   /1

JOKES TOTAL: _____ /4

Kid continue to the next page ➡️

Word Frenzy

KID

1. Noun (Article of Clothing)
2. Noun (Animal - Plural)
3. Noun (Article of Clothing)
4. Noun (Body Part)

While visiting my grandparents, Dad lost his _____ while
#1

trying to break up a fight between their _____! The las
#2

time he did that, they ate his _____ and left a scar on his
#3

_____ . I guess he only learns his lessons the hard way!
#4

/2

1. Noun (Sea Animal - Plural)
2. Verb (Ends in ED)
3. Noun (Body Part - Plural)
4. Verb (Past Tense)
5. Adjective

Last night, I dreamt my neighbor's had a mansion with a swimming

pool full of _____ . When I dove in, they all _____ !
#1   #2

Then they grew human _____ and _____ from the poc
#3   #4

Dad says I have really _____ dreams.
#5

/2

WORD FRENZY TOTAL: _____ /4

Kid continue to the next page ➡

Silly Scenarios

KID

You are the World's Smartest Dog! Using your body, teach the rest of the dogs how to stop pooping on the lawn and use the toilet... if only you could talk!

___/2

While rowing a boat, a giant octopus reaches over the side and tries to pull you into the water. Fight to stay afloat!

___/2

SILLY SCENARIOS TOTAL: ___/4

 DAD   /12
GRAND TOTAL

 KID   /12
GRAND TOTAL

ROUND CHAMPION

ROUND
10

Pass the book to Dad!

Dad Jokes

DAD

Why didn't George Washington pick up the phone when freedom called?

Because he wanted to let freedom ring.

/1

Why do so many people watch videos online during the 4th of July?

Because they're said to be so gallantly streaming!

/1

What is the Persian Gulf's favorite instrument?

Electric Qatar!

/1

What animal communicates only through the telephone?

A croco-DIAL.

/1

JOKES TOTAL: /4

Dad continue to the next page

Word Frenzy

DAD

1. Noun (Plural)
2. Adjective
3. Adjective
4. Verb

Someday, robots will control everything, even all of the

_____ in the world. They will be _____ and _____
#1   #2   #3

However, one thing robots will never be able to do is _____
                                                       #4

like my father!

_____ /2

1. Noun
2. Adjective
3. Verb

I want to get a new _____ for my birthday. They are
                    #1

underrated and can be used for so many things, such as making

my brother _____ and my parents _____ . My birthday
           #2   #3

can't come soon enough!

_____ /2

WORD FRENZY TOTAL: _____ /4

Dad continue to the next page ➡

Silly Scenarios

DAD

You're a snowman running a marathon, and you're determined to win! Unfortunately, the more you sweat, the more you melt. Try to get to the finish line!

_____ /2

You're a T-Rex that is trying to play golf. Drive, chip, and putt using your elbows as hands!

_____ /2

SILLY SCENARIOS TOTAL: _____ /4

Now, pass the book to Kid!

Kid Jokes

What's the only sport played backwards?

BACK-etball!

/1

What do you call it when neither person wins at archery?

A bow tie!

/1

What kind of rating does our solar system have on Amazon?

One star.

/1

Why are windows so good at explaining things?

They're always perfectly clear.

/1

JOKES TOTAL: _____ /4

Kid continue to the next page ➡

Word Frenzy

KID

1. Noun (Type of Food)
2. Noun (Snack – Plural)
3. Adjective
4. Noun (Thing)

Last night, I smelled _____ near the bathroom and went to go
#1

see what was going on. Turns out it was just my brother

sleepwalking and looking for his missing _____! He turned
#2

and stared at me, then whispered, "_____ _____."
#3   #4

He can be pretty weird when he sleepwalks!

_____ /2

1. Noun (Animal)
2. Verb (Past Tense)
3. Noun (Body Part)

Our _____ used to really like my Dad. But one day, my Dad
#1

accidentally _____ it's _____, and now they don't get
#2   #3

along anymore.

_____ /2

WORD FRENZY TOTAL: _____ /4

Kid continue to the next page ➡

108

Silly Scenarios

You're in choir class and you have to hum the National Anthem with your tongue stuck to the bottom of your mouth!

_____ /2

It's the windiest afternoon you've ever seen, and you have to walk 80 balloons to your Grandma's birthday party, down the street. Tie the balloons all over your body and try to walk there while you get blown in so many different directions!

_____ /2

SILLY SCENARIOS TOTAL: _____ /4

 DAD   /12

GRAND TOTAL

 KID   /12

GRAND TOTAL

ROUND CHAMPION

ROUND 11

TIE-BREAKER

Dad Jokes

DAD

What type of shoe can't make up its mind?

Flip flops.

/1

What do you call a grumpy whale?

A "Humpf" Back.

/1

What do British fish say when saluting her Majesty?

"Cod save the Queen!"

/1

Did you hear the reviews about the new Aqua Man movie?

There's something kind of fishy about the plot.

/1

JOKES TOTAL: _____ /4

Dad continue to the next page

Word Frenzy

DAD

1. Adjective
2. Noun
3. Noun
4. Proper Noun (Place)

The new city of "_____ _____" is going to be a very
         #1   #2

magical place! It will be home to the biggest _____ in the
                                                      #3

world and should attract many tourists, especially from

_____. I cannot wait to live there someday soon!
      #4

/2

1. Proper Noun (Friend's Name)
2. Adjective
3. Noun (Place)
4. Verb
5. Noun (Part of a Dog)

My friend's pet dog, _____, is very_____, so we too
                           #1   #2

her to the _____ to _____ with all the other dogs.
               #3   #4

Unfortunately, the other dogs kept sniffing her _____
                                                        #5

and ran off whimpering! I guess we didn't wash the skunk smell

off her afterall!

/2

WORD FRENZY TOTAL: _____ /4

Dad continue to the next page ➡

114

Silly Scenarios

You're riding on a motorcyle and you forgot your mask is up. Keep driving while you get bugs stuck in you mouth!

_____/2

You're a mime whose pretending to be trapped in a clear box, when a bee stings you on the forehead! Yikes, now you're stuck in the box with the bee!

_____/2

SILLY SCENARIOS TOTAL: _____/4

Now, pass the book to Kid!

Kid Jokes

Why was the fog monster let go from the basketball team?

He was all over the place and always MIST his shots!

_____ /1

Why was the bowling ball so quiet?

It liked to hear the pin drop.

_____ /1

What music did Joe listen to while picking his nose?

A little bit of boogie!

_____ /1

What happens when a humpback stubs its toe?

It whales!

_____ /1

JOKES TOTAL: _____ /4

Kid continue to the next page

Word Frenzy

KID

1. Noun (Article of Clothing)
2. Noun (Animal)

Yesterday, I got a whiff of something awful coming from the kitchen! Turns out it was just Dad washing his _____(s)
#1
in the sink. My mom says they smell like a mix of_____,
#2
cheese, and cabbage. Thank goodness I have my own bathroom!

_____ /2

1. Adjective
2. Noun (Insect - Plural)
3. Noun (Body Part - Plural)

Last night, I saw a(n)_____ monster under my bed! It was
#1
slowly eating a bowl full of _____ and wanted to share with
#2
me. My_____started to shake and I climbed under
#3
my sheets. Luckily, it was all just a dream!

_____ /2

WORD FRENZY TOTAL: _____ /4

Kid continue to the next page ➜

Silly Scenarios

You are lying in bed. When you wake up, you realize that your arms are stuck to the sides of your body, but you really have to use the bathroom. How do you do it?!

_____ /2

Auditions for Clown College are today, and you're going to impress the judges by juggling dishes... while also doing the Floss dance!

_____ /2

SILLY SCENARIOS TOTAL: _____ /4

 DAD /12
GRAND TOTAL

 KID /12
GRAND TOTAL

The Ultimate Don't Laugh Challenge Master

Check out our other joke books!

Visit us at
www.DontLaughChallenge.com
to check out our newest books!"

Made in the USA
Coppell, TX
18 March 2020